Conservative Icons: The Lives and Legacies of Ronald Reagan and Margaret Thatcher

By Charles River Editors

About Charles River Editors

Charles River Editors was founded by Harvard and MIT alumni to provide superior editing and original writing services, with the expertise to create digital content for publishers across a vast range of subject matter. In addition to providing original digital content for third party publishers, Charles River Editors republishes civilization's greatest literary works, bringing them to a new generation via ebooks.

Visit charlesrivereditors.com for more information.

Introduction

Ronald Reagan (1911-2004)

"The nine most terrifying words in the English language are: 'I'm from the government and I'm here to help.'" – Ronald Reagan

In the famous movie *Back to the Future*, Marty McFly travels back to 1955, and, in an attempt to convince his friend Doc Brown that he is from 1985, tells the 1955 version of Doc Brown that Ronald Reagan is president. Doc looks at him incredulously and laughs, chortling, "Ronald Reagan? The actor?" In a story that could have come straight out of Hollywood, the golden actor rose through California politics to become California governor and eventually the 40th President.

The 70+ year old former actor then went on to have one of the most consequential presidencies of the 20th century, unquestionably making him one of the most influential men of the last 50 years. And his name is still as relevant in American politics today, with every politician with an R next to his or her name trying to claim Ronald Reagan's conservative mantle. In the Republican presidential nomination debates in 2011, Reagan's name was invoked an average of over 5 times per debate, more than every other president combined. Meanwhile, Americans of all stripes continue to debate the merits of "Reaganomics" more than 30 years after Reagan was elected.

Like all legends, Reagan's lengthy life and career have been molded to fit certain narratives, to the point that they obscure the actual man. *Conservative Icons* looks at the personal and family life of the Golden Age actor, governor and president, while highlighting his accomplishments and assessing his ongoing political legacy. Along with pictures of Reagan and other important people and events in his life, you will learn about Reagan like you never have before, in no time at all.

Margaret Hilda Thatcher (1925-)

"Being powerful is like being a lady. If you have to tell people you are, you aren't." – Margaret Thatcher

A lot of ink has been spilled covering the lives of history's most influential figures, but how much of the forest is lost for the trees? In Charles River Editors' British Legends series, readers can get caught up to speed on the lives of Great Britain's most important men and women in the time it takes to finish a commute, while learning interesting facts long forgotten or never known.

Sir Winston Churchill is often cited as Britain's greatest prime minister for leading the United Kingdom against Hitler's Nazi war machine during World War II, and indeed he was the idol of the one person who many think might have surpassed him: Margaret Thatcher. Thatcher not only became Britain's first female prime minister, she also became its longest serving prime minister.

The political precedents Thatcher set as a woman would be enough of a legacy in its own right, but Thatcher effectively wielded her power in a way that made a lasting contribution both to geopolitics and the perception of female politicians in general. Thatcher is widely credited, along with Ronald Reagan, as one of the principal Cold Warriors who brought about the demise of the Soviet Union, whose leaders gave her the famous nickname "Iron Lady". And of course, Thatcher was recently in the spotlight again with the release of the critically acclaimed movie *The Iron Lady*, starring Meryl Streep.

With the success of that movie, Thatcher has undergone a cultural revival and re-iconization in many quarters for her political stances and political achievements. At the same time, however, the role she played as a woman is now often overlooked out of the expedience of political correctness, and it is considered uncivil to analyze Thatcher's political rise through the prism of sex. In fact, at times the former Prime Minister claimed to understand an issue better due to her sex and sometimes used her sex more subliminally

Conservative Icons details the Iron Lady's life and career, but it also humanizes her and explores the role gender played in her rise to power and ultimately her legacy. Along with pictures of important people, places, and events in his life, you will learn about Margaret Thatcher like you never have before, in no time at all.

Ronald Reagan

Chapter 1: Early Life and Education, 1911 – 1932

Midwestern Childhood

Today Ronald Reagan is intimately associated with California, both as a movie star and the state governor, but the future governor of a state sometimes called the Sunshine State was born in the middle of a blizzard. On February 6, 1911, in Tampico, Illinois, Ronald Reagan was born in his family's second story apartment, despite the severe blizzard raging outside. Reagan's parents had Irish Catholic and British heritage, with father Jack being a working salesman, a profession Reagan's older brother would also take up.

The Reagans only remained in the idyllic small town for a short time. Shortly before Reagan's 4th birthday, the family left for Chicago, where Reagan's father Jack took a job as a member of a shoe department staff. Living in Chicago also proved temporary. In his childhood, Reagan's family was itinerant due in large part to Jack. Despite the semblance of a moral all-American upbringing, Reagan's childhood was constantly disrupted by his alcoholic father. In Chicago, Jack was arrested for public drunkenness, lost his job, and was forced to leave the city. Leaving the big city behind them, the Reagans moved to a small town called Galesburg, but in 1918, they left the town for the same reasons they had had to leave Chicago. Jack's drinking problem wreaked havoc in the Reagan household.

Jack's drunkenness, however, was in stark contrast to Reagan's mother Nelle, who adhered to a strictly Protestant morality and did not drink at all. Ronald Reagan's family mirrored the cultural conflicts taking place across America. Jack was an Irish Catholic with a drinking problem, while Nelle was a prohibitionist member of the Disciples of Christ Church. Drinking was, thus, a major point of conflict in the Reagan home. In the 1920's, Americans across the country were having the same discussions, as Prohibition and speakeasies competed to win over American hearts and minds.

Ronald and his brother, Neil, grew to choose between the lives of their parents. Ronald chose to be more like his mother, adopting her faith and temperance, while Neil chose a more mischievous life, became an advertising executive, and converted to Roman Catholicism.

The Reagan family circa 1916. Jack called Ronald "Dutch" due to his "Dutchboy" haircut

Education

Since Reagan's family moved around so frequently, Ronald's early education was erratic and unstable. Nevertheless, despite changing schools, Reagan performed well in his early education, and even managed to skip a grade. His brother, on the other hand, fell behind a grade.

In high school, Reagan found his calling. In Dixon, Illinois, Reagan became active in sports and clubs. In academics, he only maintained a low-B average, but he was on varsity sports teams, school government, art clubs and volunteer organizations. He was elected president of his senior class, vice president of the Boy's Hi-Y (a moral uplift group) and was art editor of the school newspaper, the *Dixonian*. He was also a varsity football and baseball player.

Where Reagan shined most, however, was in drama. As a member of the Dramatic Club, Reagan starred in *You and I* with his high school girlfriend, Margaret Cleaver. Reagan further developed his interest in drama at Eureka College, which he began attending in 1928. Located in a small Illinois town just like those in which Reagan had grown up, Eureka College was also a center of the Disciples of Christ Church. Economic collapse, however, dominated Reagan's time in college. His family was too poor to afford tuition, but Reagan had saved enough money through working as a lifeguard and construction laborer during his high school summers. Reagan was famously credited with saving nearly 80 lives as a lifeguard, keeping track by literally notching marks on a wooden log.

By the fall of 1929, the nation was descending into the Great Depression, further complicating Reagan's ability to attend the college. Fortunately, despite dire financial times, Reagan secured an athletic scholarship that allowed him to continue at Eureka. Much like in high school, Reagan excelled in extracurriculars. He joined a fraternity, Tau Kappa Epsilon, and began to star regularly in college plays. He was also elected president of his college senior class. He graduated in 1932, though with substantial debt due to the Depression, and horrible grades – mostly D's and C's. At home, his father had been out of work for months, and his family was deep in financial distress. Despite the circumstances, Reagan managed to secure a job as a lifeguard for the summer after graduating, a sizable achievement given the state of the economy.

Chapter 2: World War II and Hollywood, 1933 – 1962

Sportscasting and Hollywood

Reagan's screen credit in *Cowboy from Brooklyn*, 1938.

After spending the summer as a lifeguard, Reagan hoped to spearhead the career he really wanted. Hoping to intertwine his love for sports with his charming charisma, Reagan wanted to be a radio sportscaster. He travelled throughout Iowa interviewing and searching for the position he wanted.

Despite a series of frustrating rejections, Reagan eventually secured a position broadcasting on radio for the University of Iowa's Hawkeyes. This position was short-lived, because Reagan became a staff member of radio station WOC in Davenport, Iowa a year later. His promotions in radio didn't stop there, however; he was later promoted to a position in Des Moines as an announcer for the Chicago Cubs. Not bad considering the nation was in the depths of the Great Depression. But that's not to say Reagan was the 1930s version of Bob Uecker. In fact, in a time before TV existed, Reagan's emotional delivery was often used to do play-by-play accounts of games that were being played elsewhere, while the descriptions of what was going on in those games were wired over to his station.

Reagan's time with the Cubs is largely forgotten, because as fate would have it, the traveling nature of that job paved the way for the profession he would later become best known for. While covering the Cubs in 1937, Reagan traveled to California, where he participated in various screentests. As a result of them, Reagan managed to secure his first position as an actor with

Warner Brothers, signing a 7 year contract and moving west permanently. It was a career-defining and life changing move.

"B List" Actor and Marriage

Reagan was so eager to get to Los Angeles that in May 1937 he completed the 1,900-mile drive from Des Moines to Los Angeles in just three days. He did so alongside thousands of refugees who were also moving west to escape the Great Dust Bowl that had devastated the nation's midsection.

When Reagan arrived in Hollywood, he quickly learned the rigid hierarchy associated with the movie-making industry. Being a relatively new and inexperienced actor, Reagan was consigned to the B-List, meaning he would participate only in low-budget films and receive smaller compensation. Regardless, Ronald was happy to be acting, and among the B-Listers, he shined. His very first role was a starring one in a film called *Love Is On the Air*. In the film's first shooting, Reagan fumbled, having difficulty with injecting emotion into material he had never seen before. He brought the lines home, memorized them overnight, and was able to perform much better in the following day's shooting. This became his practice throughout his career.

Reagan followed up *Love Is On the Air* with a slew of performances. He played everything from the title role in *Sergeant Murphy* to a lead position as a drunk playboy in *Dark Victory*. And in 1940, Reagan earned his famous nickname "the Gipper" through his performance in *Knute Rockne, All American*. His strong performance in that role ensured he would continue to carry the character's name off stage.

In 1938, Reagan starred with a woman named Jane Wyman in a film called *Brother Rat*. Wyman became infatuated with Reagan, but Reagan did not return the affection. In late 1939, however, Reagan's feelings for Wyman changed abruptly. When she was hospitalized for stomach pains, Reagan rushed to see her, and the two were engaged to marry by the time she was released.

Reagan and Wyman

The engagement and later marriage proved to be ridden with the tabloid fodder typical of Hollywood marriages. Supposedly, Wyman's hospitalization was a product of a pill overdose and was designed to render sympathy from Reagan, and coerce him into marriage. Worse, Wyman's marriage to Reagan was her third, and their engagement came while she was still settling a divorce from her second husband. Regardless, the two married in 1940, had their first child in 1941, and adopted a second in 1945.

Initially, however, marriage was to be second in Reagan's life. In December of 1941, the United States entered World War II, and Reagan was called to duty.

Service in World War II

Back in 1937, Reagan took the prerequisite tests to gain admission to the Army Enlistment Reserve. He was commissioned as a Second Lieutenant in the Office Reserves Corps of the Cavalry on May 25th, 1937.

With the outbreak of war, Reagan was not immediately called to duty. By April of 1942, however, Reagan was enrolled in active service. This came just as his acting career was booming. His success in a film called *Kings Row* had allowed his name to be floated for a lead position in the soon-to-be-famous film, *Casablanca*.

Reagan in Kings Row

In reality, though, Reagan's military service was not terribly disruptive to his career. Because he had abysmal vision – he could not read most signs just ten feet away without glasses - he was not eligible to serve abroad. He spent most of his time at the First Motion Picture Unit (FMPU), a Hollywood division of the army located in Los Angeles. There, he performed in films designed to help train recruits and prepare them for war. As far as service in World War II went, Ronald Reagan had the best possible position. The only active combat Reagan ever saw was witnessed in the comfort of a studio, aided by props and technical effects.

Despite not seeing real combat, Reagan's work was not inconsequential. The films he participated in were seen by hundreds of thousands of American military men, boosting morale and helping keep the nation's armed forces prepared for the harshest conditions. Reagan served in the FMPU almost until war's end, with his official release from active service coming in December 1945, over 3 months after Japan had surrendered.

Screen Actor's Guild, Communism, and Second Marriage

Before the war, Reagan had been elected to the Board of Directors for the Screen Actors Guild. When he returned to the guild after the war, he was quickly elected the third vice president, in 1946. During the war, Reagan joined a variety of civic groups, including the Hollywood Democratic Committee and the Hollywood Independent Citizens Committee of the Arts, Sciences and Professions. Each of these groups were left-leaning, and many consorted openly with communists. As a member, Reagan began to give political speeches. He condemned the internment of Japanese-Americans, attacked British and Dutch colonialism and opposed American support for Chiang Kai-shek, China's anti-communist leader, in that country's civil war.

On February 9, 1950, a young U.S. Senator from Wisconsin was delivering an ordinary political speech to the Republican Women's Club in Wheeling, West Virginia. But in the middle of the speech, he pulled out a piece of paper which he claimed was a list of dozens of known Communists working in the State Department. This sensational announcement by Senator Joseph McCarthy propelled him to the forefront of national politics, but anti-Communist hysteria was already years old. Shortly after World War II, Congress' House Committee on Un-American Activities began investigating Americans across the country for suspected ties to Communism.

The most famous victims of these witch hunts were Hollywood actors, such as Charlie Chaplin, whose "Un-American activity" was being neutral at the beginning of World War II, a position that had been the country's official status until 1941 and had been held by hundreds of thousands of Americans of all stripes, including a young John F. Kennedy. Of course, Reagan himself was by now a well-known Hollywood political figure. As a result, the FBI began to maintain a file on Reagan, suspecting him to be a communist sympathizer, even while the local Democratic Party urged him to run for Congress.

In 1947, Reagan was elected President of the Screen Actors Guild, which he served until 1952, and then again in 1959. His wife Jane cited his presidency as a distraction and thought her husband was becoming too political when she filed for divorce in 1948. A year later, Reagan met Nancy Davis when she approached him because her own name was being mentioned on a communist blacklist. They began dating and were married in 1952.

Nancy Reagan in 1950

The Reagans in 1964

Regardless of Reagan's daily interactions with communists, he himself was no communist. His earliest political statements were mute on the subject of communism, but as president of the Guild, Reagan came into open confrontation with communists on a regular basis. This solidified his anti-communist alignment. Throughout a series of labor disputes in the 1940's and 1950's, Reagan was left to negotiate with Hollywood leaders, communists and otherwise. He personally found the communists uncompromising and irrational.

By the late 1940's, Reagan had done a complete 360 on communism. The U.S. government, which had earlier suspected Reagan of being a communist, also shifted its position. Instead of spying on Reagan, the House Un-American Activities Committee called Reagan in to testify on the infiltration of communism in Hollywood. Though Reagan opposed communism, he continued to oppose "Red Baiting" as well, and told the Committee that he believed democratic principles trumped the panic of the Red Scare.

By the 1950's, Reagan's career as an actor was in full swing. He transitioned his focus from movies to television, and became host of *General Electric Theater*. His salary now made him fairly prosperous financially. He continued to star in television throughout the early 1960's and became a household name throughout Hollywood and much of the nation.

Chapter 3: Early Political Career and Governor, 1962-1975

"Time for Choosing"

Throughout the 1950s, Reagan remained a Democrat, but his ideological positions were gradually shifting right, spurred in part by his work at the *General Electric Theater*. The executives and corporate leaders at GE, the show's sponsor, helped inspire Reagan to shift his political disposition. Reagan's involvement with GE was not limited to *GE Theater*; he also began working on company advertisements and factory morale. As part of this, he toured GE factories across the country and became better acquainted with the values of middle America. In talking with managers, he learned of the burden of taxes and regulation on company operations.

As President of the Screen Actors Guild, Reagan had endorsed candidates for President. In '52 and '56, Reagan was an Eisenhower supporter, though he fashioned himself a "Democrat for Eisenhower." By 1960, however, Reagan supported Republican Richard Nixon against Democrat John F. Kennedy, and by the time the election of 1964 rolled around, Reagan had not only completed his shift to the right but was now closely identified with its most radical faction. Far right politicians across the country sought Reagan as a spokesperson and public supporter. These included Southern Governors Ross Barnett and Orville Faubus. Most important among these politicians, however, was Senator Barry Goldwater of Arizona. Reagan's transition from suspected communist to champion of an untouchable free market was now complete.

"Mr. Conservative", Barry Goldwater

Reagan was the Barry Goldwater Campaign Co-Chair in California in 1964. Goldwater's victory for the Republican Presidential nomination was not easy, and his eventual triumph sent tremors throughout the Republican establishment. In challenging the more moderate Eastern wing of the party, Goldwater took the reins of power away from the presumed frontrunner, Nelson A. Rockefeller. Until 1964, the moderates had dominated the GOP, but Goldwater ensured that conservatism would forever leave its mark on the Republican Party.

Ronald Reagan proved a more effective spokesman for Goldwater than the candidate himself. Reagan's charisma and down-home eloquence made him popular within the Goldwater campaign. Because Goldwater's far-right positions – opposition to civil rights legislation and the New Deal and a tough line on the Soviet Union – alienated much of middle America, Reagan, as a former Democrat, was sought to help sell Goldwater to the American people.

In a film called "Time for Choosing," Reagan articulated Goldwater's message better than the Arizona Senator himself. While Goldwater was mired in accusations of racism and extremism, Reagan turned America's attention to the size of government: "The issue in this election is whether we believe in our capacity for self-government or whether we abandon the American Revolution and confess that a little intellectual elite in a far-distant capital can plan our lives for us better than we can plan them ourselves."

Despite his eloquence, Reagan's arguments went mostly unheeded in 1964. Reagan's devout enthusiasm for Barry Goldwater was very clearly not shared by his fellow Americans; Goldwater lost to Lyndon Johnson in the biggest popular vote loss in American history, a landslide that affected Republicans across the country dragged down by Goldwater, who was perceived to be too rightwing. Amid a seeming consensus on "New Dealism" and a desire to calm racial tensions in the South, Goldwater's views were seen as far outside of the American mainstream, a theme Johnson's campaign struck on time and again. In one of the most famous and memorable political ads in American history, the "Daisy" Ad, Johnson's campaign implied that voting for Goldwater could lead to nuclear war. A similar ad would be used in 1984 by presidential candidate Walter Mondale against Ronald Reagan himself.

Despite Goldwater's shellacking, Reagan continued to believe that this brand of conservatism could appeal to middle America. Goldwater just hadn't been the ideal spokesman.

Running for Governor

Ronald Reagan wasn't the only one who thought Goldwater was simply a poor salesman of good ideas. Businessmen and Republican leaders throughout California thought Reagan could be a better leader for the conservative movement than Goldwater had been. With the Black Power movement and student protests in Berkeley at the fore of California politics, state Republicans thought Reagan was their only hope. In 1965, a group of wealthy Republican businessmen formed the "Friends of Ronald Reagan" group to draft him as a candidate to run for governor.

Initially, Reagan and his wife were reluctant. Reagan was certainly very interested in the job but was afraid it would put his family into financial distress. After shifting around some of his property, however, Reagan felt comfortable with a smaller salary if it meant he could be governor of California. Still, while many Republicans admired Reagan's charisma, they were also aware that he needed some training before he was ready to campaign. Friends of Ronald Reagan hired a political consulting firm and trained Reagan in the issues facing California to prepare him for a run. Facing the two-term incumbent Democratic Governor Pat Brown would not be easy.

Reagan was the early favorite within the Republican Party and coasted through the gubernatorial nominating process. For his part, Governor Brown was happy to face Reagan in 1966, believing him to be a weak candidate who could easily be pigeon-holed as a right-wing radical and a lightweight Hollywood actor with no political experience.

The campaign focused primarily on the student anti-Vietnam protests and Black Power violence that were pervading life in California. Reagan jumped on the growing resentment of the civil rights movement among white Californians, and he framed his campaign on a promise to restore law and order.

On Election Day, Reagan's message sold. Governor Brown's attempts to label Reagan an extremist fell flat, and Reagan won with nearly 58% of the vote.

The Reagans celebrate victory

Governor of California

Reagan took the oath of office and became governor of California on January 3rd, 1967. At 56, Reagan assumed the governorship after having spent the vast majority of his career in Hollywood.

When Reagan became governor, he took hold of a state with a massive budget deficit. During the campaign, Reagan had promised to cut and pare the cost and size of state government. Confronted with an enormous deficit, Reagan thought cutting spending made sense. He soon realized, however, that many of the cuts he desired were either politically untenable or legally impossible. It quickly became obvious that the only solution was to raise taxes. Today Republicans constantly invoke Reagan's name in support of cutting taxes and/or promising to never raise them, but Governor Reagan put his ideology aside and signed a bill authorizing the biggest tax hike in the history of any U.S. state.

Around the time Reagan came to office, abortion was quickly and heatedly becoming a national topic of contention, and it also arose during Reagan's first term in office. The legislature passed a bill allowing abortions in situations of rape, incest and when a mother's life was in danger. Reagan morally opposed abortion, but he understood the necessity of the practice in these specific situations. Despite opposition from Christian leaders, Reagan signed the bill into law. Reagan would later take a more conservative stance and say that he would have opposed the bill if he had more experience, but over 40 years later, the abortion debate still falls along the same lines.

While Reagan was still learning how to achieve parts of his political agenda, he continued to work the media masterfully. In 1968, midway through his first term, he entertained the idea of running for President. Reagan floated his name as a possible compromise candidate if the Republicans could not decide on a nominee. When the GOP selected Richard Nixon, however, Reagan withdrew his name from consideration.

Reagan's primary success in his first term came through his recurrent use of force to quell protesters on state colleges. He used similar harsh action to quiet the Black Panther Movement. Candidate Reagan had promised to restore law and order among the protesters, and Governor Reagan would make good on that promise in 1969, using police to break up the "People's Park Protests" in Berkeley. Some would criticize Reagan for the violence that came with breaking up the protests. With protests against the Vietnam War flaring the following year, Reagan remained defiant about quelling protests, telling the press there would be "no more appeasement."

In 1970, Reagan sought reelection, despite the minimal achievements of his first term. Without a conservative revolution to show for, Reagan's appeal was both broadened and limited, depending on which side of the aisle viewers sat. Liberals realized he wasn't the evildoer they suspected, while conservatives were disappointed. Regardless, Reagan won reelection with 53% of the vote, a smaller margin than he had won in 1966.

Reagan had devoted much of his reelection campaign to welfare reform. He contended that welfare was frequently given to people who didn't need it, while it failed to help those who did. In 1966 candidate Reagan had famously promised "to send the welfare bums back to work", and 5 years later, Reagan passed the Welfare Reform Act of 1971, which reduced California's welfare rolls significantly while increasing the benefits of the recipients who were still eligible.

The Welfare Reform Act proved to be the high point of the Reagan governorship. Leaving office in 1975, Reagan left behind a decidedly mixed record. His promise to drastically reduce the size of government had not come true; he had, however, restored "law and order" in California and reduced welfare dependency. With the growing Christian Right movement, Reagan also had a mixed record: he legalized some abortions in his state and signed the nation's first no-fault divorce law.

In spite of his mixed record, the charismatic Reagan remained the poster child of American conservatism. With that in mind, Reagan set his sights on the White House.

Chapter 4: Presidential Politics, 1976-1980

Challenging Gerald Ford in 1976

Reagan had garnered presidential hopes since the last years of his governorship, and with Richard Nixon winning a landslide reelection campaign in 1972, Reagan was gearing up to take on the open Republican primary in 1976.

Unbeknownst to everyone, however, Nixon's presidency unraveled in stunning fashion, beginning with events before his reelection. On the night of June 17, 1972, a security guard making the rounds at the Watergate complex in Washington D.C. discovered tape on several door latches, meant to keep the doors unlocked. The guard removed the tape only to find it there again a short time later. The security guard called the police, who found five men inside the office of the Democratic National Committee. What initially seemed like a routine burglary case was actually the beginning of one of the most bizarre scandals in American history.

Investigators immediately discovered that the men were bugging the office phones, but they were amazed to find that the five men all had connections to the Committee to Re-elect the President (CReeP). One of them, James McCord, was a former CIA employee who was on CReeP's payroll. Interrogation of the burglars and the discovery of phone numbers also exposed their connections to G. Gordon Libby and E. Howard Hunt, personal aides to President Nixon himself. When Washington Post reporters Carl Bernstein and Bob Woodward, relying on a confidential source nicknamed "Deep Throat," reported that Libby and Howard were guiding the burglars with walkie-talkies, it appeared the burglary went all the way up to the White House.

By August 1974, it was clear that Nixon was on his way to being impeached and convicted. Before being forcibly removed, Nixon became the first President to resign from office on August 8, 1974. Nixon had been indicted earlier in 1974, but new President Gerald Ford controversially pardoned him in September. 40 government officials who worked in the White House, F.B.I.,

C.I.A. and Justice Department were eventually indicted for participating in or covering up the Watergate burglaries.

Watergate and Nixon's resignation threw Reagan's plan into disarray. Gerald Ford, Nixon's successor, was now seeking reelection in 1976 as an incumbent, and if Reagan ran, it would threaten to divide the GOP and reduce its chances of victory in the general election. At the same time, Ford was vulnerable. He had already become the first person to ascend to the presidency without being elected President or Vice President (Nixon appointed Ford his new Vice President after Spiro Agnew resigned), and by offering amnesty to Vietnam War draft dodger and appointing Nelson Rockefeller Vice President, Ford alienated conservatives in the Republican Party. Reagan saw an opening for victory and thus opted to challenge the sitting Republican president.

Initially, Reagan's campaign floundered. He lost many of the early critical primaries in New Hampshire, Florida and, worst, in his state of birth, Illinois. By the campaign's second-half, however, Reagan shifted gears and began talking about foreign policy instead of taxation and welfare. Being the hot topic of the day, Reagan's perceived strength on the Soviet Union catapulted him ahead, and he began winning primary after primary. By the time of the GOP convention in July, however, neither Ford nor Reagan had enough delegates to secure the nomination. Since Ford controlled the Party apparatus after having been in Washington for decades, he was able to secure the nomination on the first ballot, by a narrow margin.

Reagan congratulates Ford at the 1976 convention

Regardless, Reagan's concession speech outshone Ford's acceptance, and was the convention's highlight. Ford went on to lose the general election, while Reagan vowed to run again. As it would turn out, Ford's loss to Jimmy Carter provided Reagan the perfect opportunity to try again.

"There You Go Again": The Election of 1980

With Jimmy Carter faltering on both domestic and foreign policy, 1980 provided the perfect opportunity for Reagan to give the presidency a second try. Carter had the misfortune of taking over the White House at the most inopportune of times, and by the end of his term, the nation was rattled by a hostage crisis, rising inflation, and sky-high oil prices.

On July 15, 1979, the United States was in the midst of another energy crisis, brought about by the revolution in Iran. President Carter decided to address the nation about the energy crisis, telling Americans that the "crisis of confidence" in the country was a "fundamental threat" to the nation. Carter was bemoaning what he viewed as the excesses and selfishness of the decade, lecturing Americans that "too many of us now tend to worship self-indulgence and consumption."

Although he never actually used the word malaise in the speech, the "malaise" speech was emblematic of Carter's pessimistic style and his habit of talking down to the nation. It was also a perfect example of why Carter had an approval rating around 35 percent at the end of the '70s. 1980 appeared ripe for Republicans to take back the White House.

In the early stages of the race for the Republican nomination, Reagan was the presumptive favorite. However, former CIA Director and Republican Chairman George H.W. Bush won the first-in-the-nation primary, Iowa, by a narrow margin. With this, the candidate claimed he had momentum and presented a credible challenge to Reagan.

Bush's momentum was short-lived. Apart from Iowa, he was only able to win a few primaries in the Northeast, particularly in his native New England. The Bush-Reagan conflict came to a head when Bush accused Reagan of practicing "voodoo economics." Bush and many moderate Republicans were doubtful about Reagan's supply-side, trickle-down plan. The Republican electorate, however, was sold, and Reagan swept most of the country in the contest. He later chose Bush as his vice presidential running mate, hoping to patch up intra-party differences and add foreign policy bona fides to the ticket.

The general election was only slightly more challenging for Reagan. He occasionally made gaffes or misstatements, suggesting, for example, that most pollution was caused by trees and vegetation. He also failed to identify the President of France. But Americans were definitively sold after the one debate between Reagan and Carter. In the most memorable moment of the election, Carter began hammering Reagan's record on Medicare during the debate, prompting

Reagan to parry the attack completely by responding, "There you go again." The coy phrase turned Carter's attack on Carter himself, regardless of its merits and substance. Recognizing its effectiveness, Reagan would use it frequently during his presidency in other settings, including the 1984 election.

Reagan ultimately sealed the deal by stressing the question of "are you better off today than you were when President Carter took office?" With the vast majority of Americans loudly asserting that they were not better off than they were four years ago, Reagan won the election handedly with 44 states or 489 electoral votes. Doc Brown wouldn't have believed it in 1955, but America had just elected a former Hollywood actor President of the United States.

Chapter 5: Reagan's Presidency, 1981-1989

Reagan's Inaugural Address

Inauguration, Assassination Attempt, and a Tax Cut

Reagan was sworn in on January 20th, 1981, at the age of 69, becoming the oldest person sworn in as President in history. Despite Carter's "malaise" speech, Americans living in the '70s did not have a sense of doom and gloom. When President Reagan took office, he effectively captured the national mood. In his first inaugural address, Reagan acknowledged the challenges ahead, but he exuded sunny optimism, telling Americans, "I believe we, the Americans of today, are ready to act worthy of ourselves, ready to do what must be done to ensure happiness and liberty for ourselves, our children and our children's children."

Reagan's comments in his inaugural address were classic examples of his faith in free markets and smaller government, the central beliefs of his conservative political philosophy. But the "Great Communicator" had also skillfully tied his personal beliefs into a message meant to encourage Americans to rely on themselves, not government.

In style, Reagan quickly set up a unique way of managing the White House. In contrast to Carter's micromanagement, and recognizing his own comfort level as an actor, Reagan decided that he would perform theatrics while his advisors made policy, essentially making him a salesman. Reagan polished his public appearances, and offered an image of a strong White House, while his subordinates got to work making policy. In fact, Reagan was said to be bored and inattentive at White House meetings.

With this style, Reagan quickly assumed the title of "Great Communicator." Regardless of whether he was actually bored with the meat of these policies, the President seemed to have an intuitive grasp of public leadership, and Reagan masterfully utilized it to his political advantage.

On March 30th, 1981, however, Reagan's leadership was very nearly brought to an abrupt end. Less than 70 days into his term, the President was leaving a Hilton hotel when an unstable man named John Hinckley Jr. was able to get within 15 feet of the President as he approached a waiting limousine. Hinckley fired off several rounds, one of which hit press secretary James Brady in the head and another which hit Thomas Delahanty as Delahanty moved to protect Reagan. As Secret Service agents pushed Reagan into the limousine, Hinckley fired a few more rounds, one of which hit agent Timothy McCarthy in the chest as he laid across Reagan. The 6th and final round Hinckley fired bounced off the limousine's armored sidings and entered Reagan's body under his left arm, coming within an inch of his heart. Reagan was not even initially aware that he was injured until collapsing in the limousine, and he was rushed into surgery. He was released on April 11th, making a quick recovery and becoming the first sitting U.S. President to survive being shot.

Due in part to the assassination attempt, Reagan's popularity skyrocketed to a 73% approval rating. In the summer following the attempt, Reagan vowed to fulfill one of his major campaign promises: a tax cut. Reagan's supply-side plan called for a three-phase tax cut and sharp reductions in spending on social programs such as health, housing and education. The President contended that cutting taxes would free up money for business owners to increase the supply of goods and hire more employees. In late July, Congress passed the Economic Recovery Tax Act of 1981, reducing income tax rates across the board. The total cut represented a 23% reduction on the nationwide tax burden.

Sandra Day O'Connor and the Air Traffic Control Strike

During the campaign, Reagan promised to appoint a woman to the Supreme Court if there was an opening. His opportunity arose in the summer of 1981, and Reagan made an historic move by nominating Sandra Day O'Connor to the Supreme Court. While Democrats and women's groups were thrilled, conservative Republicans had reservations. Would O'Connor be willing to overturn *Roe v. Wade,* the landmark case that had legalized abortion? Despite the less-than-warm reception from Republicans, O'Connor was confirmed by a 99-0 vote in the Senate. She quickly assumed the position of a moderate judge, much as conservatives had suspected and feared.

Justice O'Connor

On August 3rd, the President was confronted with his first major crisis. The Professional Air Traffic Controllers Organization (PATCO) went on strike that morning, threatening to bring all of the nation's air traffic to a halt. In the 1980 election, PATCO had been one of the few unions to support Reagan. Reagan himself had been a union president at the Screen Actors Guild, which made him the only president to have ever been part of a union. To a point, he sympathized with striking workers.

However, the PATCO workers were public workers, employed by the federal government. Federal law expressly forbade strikes by federal employees of "critical industries." Reagan thus refused to negotiate with the strikers, and told them to return to work within 48 hours or lose their jobs. Reagan was committed to following the law.

Two days later, only 38% of the workers returned to their jobs. Reagan fired the rest. Nearly two-thirds of Americans supported the move, and the firing burnished Reagan's image as a strong and assertive leader. Many union leaders, however, thought the President was unsympathetic to the plight of workers.

Star Wars and Korean Air

Today Reagan is often cited as the president who won the Cold War, but in 1981 he was criticized by the Soviets and some Americans for escalating tensions between the two sides. His most famous comment on the Soviet Union was in his description of it as an "evil empire", and Reagan initially vowed to take an aggressive stance that would ensure the United States maintained a superior strategic capability. That Fall, Reagan ratcheted up the U.S.-Soviet arms race by announcing an ambitious defense program. It called for the development of stationary MX missiles and B-1 bombers. In December, Congress approved the biggest peace-time military budget in history, providing nearly $200 billion for military spending for fiscal year 1982.

Just over a year later, Reagan proposed a course of action that would throw off the intricate nuclear balance between East and West and tilt it in America's favor. Reagan proposed a Strategic Defense Initiative (SDI) that has come to be more popularly known as Star Wars. The program attempted to develop a laser-operated missile defense system that could intercept enemy missiles launched at U.S. targets. It got its playful name from the hope of proponents that it would one day be able to destroy enemy missiles and warheads from outer space.

SDI was controversial. While Reagan and his supporters thought it evidenced Americans strength, opponents thought it threatened to push the Soviet Union to the brink of something drastic. The nuclear balance "detente" had been the framework that guaranteed peace between the two nations for decades; developing SDI threatened to reduce the geopolitical significance of the Soviet nuclear arsenal, potentially leading to war. Reagan, however, viewed the Cold War differently than his predecessors. He proposed to *defeat* the Soviet Union, not just provide a counterweight to it.

In early 1983, Soviet-American relations deteriorated further when the Soviets shot down a Korean Air Lines flight, killing all passengers, including 61 Americans. Reagan denounced the move as a massacre and banned air traffic from the Soviet Union into the United States. Once again, Americans saw the President exerting strength in the face of the Soviet Union.

Beirut and the Invasion of Grenada

In 1975, Lebanon was turned into a battleground for several Middle Eastern nations. Although it is referred to as the Lebanon Civil War, the country had Shiite militias, Sunni militias, Christian militias, Syrian forces, Israeli forces and the Palestine Liberation Organization (PLO) all engaged in combat, with different alliances loosely connecting some of the groups together. After the Israelis had pulled out in the late '70s, they invaded Lebanon in 1982 to go after the PLO, which was using Lebanon as a staging ground for attacks across the Israeli border. Reagan initially supported Israel, hoping the invasion would keep Lebanon from being controlled by Muslim radicals who were closely allied with the Soviet Union.

Under a UN agreement, American, French, and Italian troops arrived in Lebanon to oversee the withdrawal of PLO forces from the country. In return, Israel agreed to stop shelling the country. To the international community's disappointment, however, Israel resumed its invasion of Beirut. Lebanese Christians then begin massacring hundreds of Palestinians settled in refugee camps. Reagan came under fire for his initial support of Israel's invasion, and his Secretary of State resigned over an agreement. Secretary of State Haig was quickly replaced by George Shultz. It was a low moment in Reagan's first term.

Matters in Lebanon only got worse, however. Some U.S. Marine Corps members remained stationed in Beirut on a peacekeeping mission. The Islamic militant groups had more in store. On October 23, 1983, a suicide bomber drove a hijacked truck into the U.S. Marine barracks at Beirut's airport, blowing himself and the truck up inside the building. When rescuers converged on the rubble, they were subjected to sniper fire. Nearly 250 Americans lay dead, making it the deadliest day for the military since Vietnam. Another suicide bomber destroyed the French forces' building, killing over 50. In response, Reagan authorized the marines to begin shelling Muslim stations around Beirut. Reagan had committed the country to an all-out war in Lebanon.

The mission was enormously unpopular at home. After a car bomb attacked the American embassy in the country, Congress threatened to use the War Powers Act of 1973 to force the President to withdraw all forces from Lebanon. Reagan, realizing the unpopularity of the mission, agreed to transfer the Marines from Lebanon to a naval base in the Mediterranean. The strong Reagan Presidency had suffered a major chink in its armor.

Around the same time – on October 25th, 1983 – Prime Minister Maurice Bishop of Grenada was assassinated by pro-Marxist rebels. Reagan deployed military forces to the island country on the same day, citing concerns over the 1,000 American students studying there. The invasion, however, was part of Reagan's policy to militarily confront communism wherever it threatened to spread. The invasion of Grenada was militarily much more successful than Lebanon, with the U.S. installing a pro-American government in weeks. In terms of popularity, the move boosted Reagan at home but further tarnished his international appeal. Even Prime Minister Margaret Thatcher, a strong Reagan ally, condemned the invasion. The U.S. had to veto a resolution at the U.N. condemning the Grenada action.

"It's Morning Again in America"

By the beginning of 1984, Reagan was gearing up for reelection on uncertain terms. Throughout most of Reagan's first term, supply-side economics had failed to deliver an improved economy. Unemployment was highest in early 1983, at nearly 11%, the highest since the Great Depression. In many ways, the early 1980's represented a nadir in the country's economic history. Even bank failures – unheard of since the Great Depression – occurred in 1982. The Federal budget deficit was also at an all-time peacetime high. As a result of the economic tumult, Reagan's popularity was in decline, and the Democrats picked up seats in Congress in the 1982 midterm elections.

By November of 1984, however, the economy brightened and it became "morning again in America." The unemployment rate was in steady decline, though by November it was still above 7%. Interests rates had fallen from all-time highs. In a compromise with Congress, Reagan agreed to both close tax loopholes and raise some taxes to combat the budget deficit. With each of these economic successes, Reagan's popularity improved significantly. He asked Americans the same question he had asked in 1980: "Are you better off today than you were four years ago?"

Actions speak louder than words, even for great communicators. Reagan's speeches and "Morning in America" campaign ad worked because of results. In the Cold War, Reagan managed to strike a balance between tough and conciliatory. He famously called the Soviet Union an "evil empire," but he also negotiated reductions in each country's nuclear arsenals. Reagan's conservative philosophy was most apparent in his economic policies. He lowered tax rates in his first year, deregulated the economy, and increased defense spending. Reaganomics appeared to be working by 1984.

In 1984, Reagan faced former Vice President Walter Mondale of Minnesota. At many points, the campaign focused on Reagan's age. While Reagan was already the oldest president in history, at 73 he was vying to be an even older president. The media portrayed Reagan as a senile old man, but Reagan, in a masterful quip, refuted all of his detractors in a presidential debate. In response to a question about his age, Reagan famously pledged that "I will not make age an issue of this campaign. I will not exploit, for political purposes, my opponent's youth and inexperience." Much like "there you go again", Reagan had permanently disarmed his opponent of a potential attack angle.

Reagan's campaign also ran one of the most famous and effective political ads in American history that year. Known as the "Morning in America" ad, it began with pictures of Americans heading to work while a narrator tells viewers it was morning again in America. The narrator talks about how well the economy is doing, how low interest rates are, and how many people will get married that day. As pictures of smiling Americans flash across the screen, the narrator notes the country is "prouder and stronger and better." The advertisement personified Reagan's sunny demeanor and positive tone, focusing on the accomplishments of the administration and its confidence in the direction the country was going. At the same time, it ended with a subtle jab tying Mondale to Jimmy Carter's unpopular administration, while managing not to come across like an attack ad.

With that, Reagan was set to win. On election night, he outdid his 1980 return by winning every state in the union except Mondale's home state of Minnesota. With 525 electoral votes, Reagan's reelection was one for the history books.

Reagan and Gorbachev

A new, younger, and entirely different Soviet premier came to power in 1985. After the deaths of two Soviet leaders in the early 1980's, Reagan had been unable to form lasting relationships with any of his Soviet counterparts. In March of 1985, as Reagan was beginning his second term, Mikhail Gorbachev was at the dawn of his reign in Moscow.

Gorbachev signaled a change in Soviet priorities, even suggesting he was open to unilateral arms reductions. Reagan thus hoped to meet Gorbachev in person. Soviet and American heads of state had not met face-to-face since 1979, but Reagan and Gorbachev proposed to change that, starting with a first conference in Geneva in November 1985.

Reagan meets with Gorbachev

The results of the Geneva Conference were significant. While no tangible agreement came out of the talks, the two leaders set up a plan to meet three more times: once in Reykjavik, once in Washington and a final time in Moscow. By the final meeting in Moscow, the war that had divided the world for decades was nearing its end.

The Challenger Disaster

Before Reagan and Gorbachev could meet again to discuss the nuclear arms race, the U.S. was hit with a series of crises. First among them was the worst accident in the history of American space exploration.

On the morning of January 28, 1986, the Space Shuttle Challenger launched for the 10th time, beginning Space Shuttle Program mission STS-51-L. Since 1981, NASA's space shuttles had already successfully completed 24 missions, and no American spacecraft had ever failed to reach orbit during a manned mission. The night before the launch, it was unseasonably cold in Florida, which worried some engineers at Morton Thiokol, Inc. The company was responsible for the plastic O-rings used to seal the solid rocket boosters on the space shuttle, and the engineers were worried that if the weather was too cold, the O-rings could become too stiff to properly seal the boosters.

It was a warning NASA didn't want to hear. The management team at Morton Thiokol didn't want to hear it either. They approved of launching the Challenger the following morning, assuring NASA that secondary O-rings would seal if the primary ones failed.

The next morning was cold, with temperatures just over freezing. About 75 seconds into the launch, one of the plastic O-rings failed to seal a joint in one of the solid rocket boosters, causing a breach of hot gas. The gas immediately spread to the other rocket booster and the external fuel tank, causing an explosion of the boosters, the fuel tank, and the space shuttle at nearly 50,000 feet in the air. Every astronaut onboard was killed.

The *Challenger* disaster set back NASA and the space program by two years.

The *Challenger* explosion

Libya and Iran Contra

Months later, after Muslim terrorism had plagued the U.S., Reagan ordered the air force to conduct raids in Libya, where the nation's leader, Colonel Gaddafi, was suspected of harboring terrorists. Gaddafi remained defiant after the attacks, continuing to use his bombed structures, and in 1988, Libyan terrorists were responsible for the bombing of Pan Am Flight 103 over Lockerbie, Scotland, killing 270 people.

Reagan's second term faced its greatest crisis, however, during the Iran-Contra scandal of late 1986. In 1984, the Boland Amendment had passed through Congress and expressly banned the U.S. government from giving aid to the Contras in Nicaragua, a group of anti-communist rebels fighting the Sandinista government there. In secret, however, the Reagan administration continued to give aid to the Nicaraguan Contras. It did so by selling arms to Iran, and sending the proceeds to Nicaragua. These transactions were in direct conflict with federal law.

The public learned of the Iran-Contra Affair through an *Associated Press* article in November of 1986. Reagan, however, professed to be unaware of the transactions happening within his White House. This may, in fact, have been true: the President's hands-off style meant he delegated a lot of responsibility and authority to his staff. Regardless, the public held Reagan accountable, and his approval rating plummeted by nearly 20 points within a week.

Realizing the public relations disaster, Reagan, only after initial hesitancy, took responsibility for the scandal. He fired his National Security Advisor and his assistant. The scandal quickly subsided and Reagan's popularity recovered, giving the President the nickname "Teflon President," because scandals never stuck to him for long.

Nearing the End of the Cold War

While the Iran-Contra Scandal blemished Reagan's Cold War bona fides, he managed to rapidly revive them throughout 1987 and 1988. Talks with Gorbachev had resumed around the time of the Iran-Contra crisis, in October of 1986, in Reykjavik, Iceland. But discussions in Reykjavik quickly collapsed, and the two leaders were unable to come to any agreements on arms reduction.

Before meeting with Gorbachev a third time in December of 1987, Reagan travelled to Berlin. There, in a speech at the Berlin Wall, Reagan pronounced: "General Secretary Gorbachev, if you seek peace, if you seek prosperity for the Soviet Union and Eastern Europe, if you seek liberalization, come here to this gate. Mr. Gorbachev, open this gate. Mr. Gorbachev, Mr. Gorbachev, *tear down this wall.*" The statement was controversial within the Administration itself, with many fearing that it would tarnish Reagan's relationship with Gorbachev and increase tensions again at a time when the two sides were trying to reach strategic arms limitations treaties. Ultimately, Reagan decided to leave it in because he liked it.

Reagan speaking at the Berlin Wall

After the forceful speech, Reagan and Gorbachev met in Washington in December 1987. This meeting yielded greater results. Together, the two signed the Intermediate Range Nuclear Forces Treaty, and the two countries agreed to remove *all* 2600 medium-range missiles they had stationed in Europe. It was the first arms treaty that reduced the nation's two nuclear arsenals.

Having come to an unprecedented agreement, Reagan travelled to Moscow in 1988 for his final meeting with Gorbachev. American-Soviet relations had changed significantly. Instead of being greeted as an enemy, Reagan was adorned as a celebrity in Russia. A year later, the Berlin Wall fell, the Cold War was declared over, and within just a few years, the Soviet Union collapsed entirely. Reagan's commitment to defeating – not just negotiating with – the Soviet Union had come to fruition. Whether it was Reagan's doing, however, remains a point of debate. While the president put enormous diplomatic pressure on the Soviets, the nation's collapsed from internal strife, not external aggression.

The War on Drugs

Drugs had been on the government's radar for much of the 20th century, but they were widely used and viewed as recreational during the '60s and '70s. That changed during the Reagan presidency.

Though nobody could mistake her speaking skills for her husband's, Nancy Reagan coined one of the most famous slogans of the decade when asked by a young girl at an Oakland school what she should do if somebody offered her drugs. The First Lady responded, "Well, you just say no."

"Just Say No" instantly became the slogan for the Regan Administration's "War on Drugs."

Though memorable, "Just Say No" is often viewed derisively today, and Americans in subsequent decades found "Just Say No" somewhat silly. Drug use in the United States went down substantially during the '80s, but "Just Say No" seemed like a naïve response to a problem that involved addictive drugs. On top of it, the "Just Say No" campaign, which was trying to make it cool to say no to drugs, was being led by a grandmother and other authority figures telling kids what they shouldn't do. Of course, no kid or young adult has ever thought their elders were cool.

Leaving Office

Reagan's presidency has sometimes been labeled the "Reagan Revolution," because his popularity indicated a conservative shift in the country's politics. Lyndon Johnson's "Great Society" policies, with government as people's benefactor, had dominated the nation for nearly two decades, but now Reagan had assured Americans that "government is the problem." Reagan was very popular when he left office, and the Reagan Revolution marked an ideological departure from the Great Society. A plurality of Americans has identified themselves as conservatives ever since, and Reagan's name is constantly invoked by today's Republicans as the model conservative.

Chapter 6: Later Life and Death, 1989-2004

Reagan's Vice President, George H.W. Bush, was elected President in November 1988. At age 77, Reagan left the Office of President on January 20th, 1989. Despite being the oldest person to ever leave the White House, Reagan's post-presidency was longer than many, as he lived for another 15 years.

Those 15 years, however, would be difficult ones for the elderly Reagan. He continued to make public appearances occasionally throughout the early 1990's, with his final appearance being Richard Nixon's 1994 funeral. But that year would be a devastating one for Reagan. Diagnosed with the incurable Alzheimer's Disease, Reagan issued a handwritten letter to the public explaining the diagnosis, "I have recently been told that I am one of the millions of Americans who will be afflicted with Alzheimer's Disease... At the moment I feel just fine. I intend to live the remainder of the years God gives me on this earth doing the things I have always done... I now begin the journey that will lead me into the sunset of my life. I know that for America there will always be a bright dawn ahead. Thank you, my friends. May God always bless you."

Reagan spent the remaining years of his life battling the disease, and his wife Nancy ensured that her husband was kept out of the public eye, explaining that "Ronnie would want people to remember him as he was." His mental capacity had deteriorated significantly, and he was able to recognize few people. It's been alleged that at the time of his death in 2004, the former president had no recollection of having lived in the White House.

Reagan died of pneumonia on June 5th, 2004, at the age of 93. President George W Bush declared June 11th a national day of mourning. A state funeral was given to the former president, with many notable public figures attending, including Mikhail Gorbachev and Margaret Thatcher.

Reagan's casket lies in state in the Capitol

Chapter 7: Reagan's Legacy

Reagan's death came at a point when his legacy was of politically-heated importance. President Bush had loudly embraced Reagan's legacy in his political rhetoric after Reagan left the White House, and since 1989 the Republican Party as a whole has looked to the former president as their standard bearer, with mixed results.

Reagan is often championed as the ultimate conservative today, which does a disservice to the man. Particularly on economics, Reagan's ideology of reduced government dependency, lower taxes and supply-side theories has come to define the modern Republican Party. But do modern Republicans understand Reagan for what he actually was, or have they created a mythologized and heavily exaggerated figure? This is the contention not only of Reagan opponents, but of many moderate Republicans. Today's Republican Party lauds the benefits of tax cuts, reduced government spending and social conservatism, but Reagan's record both as President and Governor suggest he was more willing to compromise than his contemporaries recall. As Governor of California, Reagan signed a historic tax *increase*. Even as President, after initially signing an unprecedented tax cut, Reagan backtracked and raised taxes to counter deficits. On government spending, the total size of government increased under Reagan's watch as well. The free-market parade, evidently, was led by Reagan through speeches more than through actions.

Another part of the modern Republican Party's coalition, the Christian Right, views Reagan with more reverence than reality. While Reagan certainly courted the Christian Right as an important element of the GOP coalition, he was not really *of* the Christian Right. He was, after all, a Hollywood actor who married another twice-divorced actress, got a divorce himself, remarried to the Astrology-believing Nancy Davis, signed a no-fault divorce law in California, and legalized abortion in that state as well. Reagan's personal associations with the Christian Right were tepid at best. He was more comfortable with Hollywood big shots than Southern Baptist Preachers.

Regardless, on both accounts – economics and social policy – the Republican Party has created an image of Reagan as a free-market Christian Crusader, a legacy that lives on more strongly in words than actions. But imagined legacies are not necessarily less important than real ones. What has been the impact of Reagan the free-market Christian on post-Reagan American politics?

Certainly the Reagan mythology helped catapult the Republican Party out of its post-World War II abyss. In 1994, the Republicans captured a majority in the House for the first time in decades and held them. In some sense, Bill Clinton's Democratic Presidency was heavily influenced by Reagan, with a welfare reform bill similar to something Reagan would have championed as its landmark achievement. The following President, George W. Bush, took the Reagan mantra and put it on steroids, slicing and dicing taxes and social spending while rapidly increasing defense spending and military engagements in the Middle East. Reagan's influence continues to be felt in American politics, even if it is a projection of a Ronald Reagan that existed more in myth than fact.

With the financial collapse of 2008 and that year's presidential election, however, the Reagan legacy was thrown quickly into question, and remains unsettled today. What role did free-marketism of the Reagan variety play in spearheading the crisis? Was the interventionism in the Middle East wise? The late 2000's diminished Republican electoral strength, though it resurged in a big way in 2010. With a presidency only decades past, Reagan's legacy remains fluid. The results of the 2012 presidential election will help shed further insight into his place in history.

For the time, though, a few things are clear: Reagan, as President, injected an unfounded sense of optimism into a country that sorely needed it. He positioned his country to hold an upper hand over its opponent superpower, and ultimately to become the one and only superpower. While this happened on Reagan's watch, the verdict remains unsettled on whether this was Reagan of Gorbachev's prerogative. Regardless, though, Presidents are remembered largely for the accomplishments that take place while they occupy the White House. In Reagan's case, the nation's economic health improved while it won a decades-long international struggle. That, along with Republicans casting him as the party's standard bearer, ensures that Reagan's legend will continue to live on.

Bibliography

Brinkley, Alan and Davis Dyer. *The American Presidency: The Authoritative Reference.* New York: Houghton Mifflin, 2004.

Collins, Robert M. *Transforming America: Politics and Culture During the Reagan Years.* New York: Columbia University Press, 2007.

Tygiel, Jules. *Ronald Reagan and the Triumph of American Conservatism.* New York: Pearson
    Education, 2006.

Wilentz, Sean. *The Age of Reagan: A history, 1974-2008.* New York: Harper Perennial, 2008.

Margaret Thatcher

What Made Thatcher Thatcher?

Thatcher's Birthplace

For a woman destined to blaze a new trail and become a trendsetter closely followed and mimicked in places around the world, Margaret Hilda Roberts actually grew up with a relatively modest background. Along with older sister Muriel, Margaret's childhood years were spent in Grantham, living above one of the two grocery stores owned by her father, Alfred Roberts. Described by Muriel as "always a Liberal at heart", Alfred was fairly active in his church and in local politics, eventually becoming a town Alderman. More importantly, Alfred firmly instilled both church and state in his young daughter.

By her teenage years, Margaret was very active in all facets of life, credited as a hard worker who excelled at everything from playing the piano to swimming. Most notably, she showed a keen interest in the sciences, which in the first half of the 20th century was almost universally viewed as a man's domain. Margaret Robers was already proving traditional gender roles would not be insurmountable barriers.

A chemist prior to becoming a barrister specializing in tax and financial matters (not, by any means, the "softer" side of law with demanding schedules), Thatcher had always been in androcentric environments. Even the choice to be a barrister in the elite and elitist male world reflects her can-do indomitable spirit at an early age. This was the early part of the 20th century, after all. The feminist revolution and attending legal, social, cultural and economic changes had not yet taken place. As the daughter of a grocer, Thatcher had grown up in such an environment and had developed the repartee and made her peace with being the only woman, often, in such situations. She also learned how to win effectively in such environments.

Astute observers have noted that "[o]rdering Aquascutum to revamp her entire wardrobe, she had her skirts pulled up, her décolleté lowered, and began showing more of her good legs. During Question Time, I noticed she would often rub the back of one black-stockinged calf with the other foot, presumably for the delectation of the frontbenchers sitting behind her."[1] Constantly underestimated and then surpassing the expectations in part *because* of this chronic underestimation of her professional and intellectual competence, Thatcher learned to walk a very fine line.

Even more than her erudition or professional competence, what was most underestimated — due mainly to stereotypes — was Thatcher's capacity for leadership. And her take-no-prisoners approach was so polarizing, so unexpected, so shocking, given her otherwise stereotypically feminine features such as her soft voice in her earlier years and mannerisms and clothes all her

---

[1] G. Sheehy, "The Sexy Side of Maggie: How Thatcher Used Her Softer Quality," *The Daily Beast*, Jan. 11, 2012, *available at* <www.thedailybeast.com/articles/2012/01/09/the-sexy-side-of-maggie-how-thatcher-used-her-softer-quality.html>.

life, that this misdirected her critics in a way that Thatcher later was able to capitalize upon. The famous British polemic Christopher Hitchens once observed that "she calmly destroyed and (if you will pardon the expression) dismembered all her male rivals, from Sir Geoffrey Howe to Nigel Lawson to Sir Ian Gilmour to Jim Prior, as well as a succession of Labour challengers."[2]

A clear indicator of Thatcher's growing sense of self-confidence and her feeling of what political dominance entails, even her voice became lower and more authoritative, possibly due to coaching and almost certainly due to her own conscious need to recalibrate her strategy. But none of these traits and no amount of evolution would have been successful had Thatcher not had "powerful sexuality," combined with a hunger for power, of change, and of being the epicentre of the moment.[3] This is Margaret Thatcher's story and within it is the evolving saga of a certain kind of British woman. For the purposes of this story, whether or not Thatcher was indeed a "feminist" (as if that label confers some magical powers or authority) is a happy enigma left to others to determine to his or her own satisfaction.

A Political Career Like No Other

When Thatcher was elected Member of Parliament (MP) for Finchley in 1959, not many powerful women politicians existed anywhere in the world. The Queen, as a head of state, was a notable exception, but she was also obviously not a political leader. Historically, women in politics had either been like Agrippina, who had tried to control the Roman Empire through sex; Lucrezia Borgia, who effectuated the fall of dynasties and kingdoms; or Queen Elizabeth I, whose sexual magnetism nonetheless earned her the stigma of being barren. Other than Elizabeth I, none were leaders in their own right, confronted directly with the great issues of the day. Thatcher would have to invent her own political future — and her identity.

When Thatcher began her political career, she was still in her mid-20s, running in 1950 and 1951 as a Conservative in Dartford, a safely held seat for the Labour party. Even then, she was noted primarily for the novelty she represented, both as the youngest and only female candidate in the race. During that time, she also married millionaire Denis Thatcher, who helped support both her political career and legal career. A self-described "honest-to-God right-winger", Denis was also a valuable source of political support for his wife, who agreed with him on nearly every issue.

---

[2] C. Hitchens, "The Iron Lady's Sex Appeal"
[3] A. Burgess, "On Sex and Politics and the Charms of Mrs. Thatcher," Vanity Fair, May 1985, *available at* <http://www.vanityfair.com/culture/features/1985/05/margaret-thatcher-198505> [A. Burgess, "Charms of Mrs. Thatcher"] ("There was a sexual aura which owed something to the cunning coiffure, the smile of sound teeth, the discreet makeup, the newly fined down figure, the unaggressive chic. But such an aura can never be solely the product of the dietician's or the beautician's art. You either have strong sexuality or you haven't.").

The Thatchers in 1984

After spending the middle half of the 1950s raising her young children and steering clear of politics, the adroit Margaret began her political career anew near the end of the decade, this time opting to run for the Finchley seat, a safe Conservative seat in the House of Commons. After winning a bitterly contested campaign, MP Thatcher began a meteoric ascent, taking just 2 years to become Undersecretary at the Ministry of Pensions and National Insurance. She spent the 1960s becoming one of the most forceful spokesmen in her party.

Edward Heath appointed Thatcher Secretary of State for Education and Science in his 1970 government, for a handful of reasons. First and possibly foremost, Heath appointed her partly to include and thus to subdue a potential rival, but the appointment was also made in part because her wing of the Tory Party was strong and non-negotiable in demanding Thatcher's role in the Cabinet. Moreover, the appointment could also be attributed to Thatcher's sheer competence and brilliance, which political rivals grudgingly admired.

Heath (left), pictured with Queen Elizabeth and the Nixons

In 1975, Thatcher defeated Heath in the internal Tory Party leadership election and became Leader of the Opposition, in the process becoming the first woman ever to lead a major political party in the United Kingdom. She became prime minister after winning the 1979 general election.

How did this happen? Many members of the British electorate had become unhappy with the post-war "statist consensus" that, in the eyes of some, took free-market autonomy and economic freedom away from the market and placed it with the State. Economic moderates favoured a pluralism of power repositories that neither Labour nor Mrs. Thatcher's Tories exactly delivered. Nonetheless what did seem to matter was that while Labour policies had been rejected, Mrs. Thatcher's policies or her leadership had not been tried yet. The British public was longing for something new. Thatcher's vision of a society with greater economic aspirations for the next generation, along with her own immense charisma, won the day.

Upon becoming Prime Minister, Margaret Thatcher introduced several political and economic initiatives to reverse what economists called "stagflation" and in common political-speak what

Thatcher and many others saw as the United Kingdom's precipitous decline. Her political and economic policies stressed deregulation and the truncating of red tape (particularly of the financial sector), increasing international competitiveness, free market supply-side economics, tax decreases, adaptable labour markets, the privatization of erstwhile state-owned commercial enterprises and other public industry, artificial adjusting of the money supply to reduce inflation, and diminishing both the hard power (legal authority) and soft power (influence) of trade unions.

Even great politicians are subject to the times. Thatcher's popularity during her first several years in office decreased due to recession and high unemployment, until economic recovery and the 1982 Falklands War returned support. Thatcher was re-elected in 1983 and then for a third term in 1987, but her Community Charge (known as "poll tax")[4] was strongly and widely repudiated by the public, and her uncompromising views on the European Community were not shared by many, including several others in her own Cabinet. Just as Thatcher's rise was facilitated by her sex, so was her downfall. For an aggressive female political leader like Thatcher, second acts were not allowed. The novelty had worn out, and Thatcher left office in 1990.

From Thatcher's ashes emerged a lame-duck Tory Party under John Major's leadership from 1990 to 1997. After Major came the Labour Party dominance of Tony Blair and Gordon Brown. Thatcher's legacy was that, in her wake, even the Labour governments — much to the annoyance of leftists — followed "Thatcher-lite" programs, having rejected their *own* traditionally leftist tax and spend programs. Especially as to public attitudes concerning the British "independent nuclear deterrent,…Scotland's devolution, and…European integration" Labour largely continued to the course laid down by the Thatcher era.[5] The public wanted to stay the course; the pull of *path-dependency* had been too strong.[6]

The public appetite had not had room enough for a Margaret Thatcher the fallen and fallible *woman* Prime Minister, but many of her attitudes and approaches, if not the fine details of her policies, proved to have durability and staying power. Would the notoriously prejudiced (at the time) Tories or the general public have expressed greater patience for a male politician who had been generally successful and had the experience factor as an asset? Likely so. Social scientist after social scientist will attest that the public image of male leaders allows them to fail out in the open in ways that female leaders just are not allowed.[7] Male leaders often are allowed to be just

---

[4] The tax was introduced in Scotland in 1989 and in England and Wales in 1990. Politically, it proved to be disastrous for Mrs. Thatcher.

[5] A. F. Heath, et al., THE RISE OF NEW LABOUR: PARTY POLICIES AND VOTER CHOICES 60-61 (Oxford University Press, 2001).

[6] *Id.*, at 61.

[7] J. Baxter, THE LANGUAGE OF FEMALE LEADERSHIP 64 *et seq.* (Palgrave MacMillan, 2010)(exploring how "senior women have to carry out extra 'linguistic work' to make their mark in the boardroom"); K. Jironet, FEMALE LEADERSHIP: MANAGEMENT, JUNGIAN PSYCHOLOGY, SPIRITUALITY AND THE GLOBAL JOURNEY THROUGH PURGATORY (Routledge, 2010); A. S. Wharton, THE SOCIOLOGY OF GENDER: AN INTRODUCTION TO THEORY

leaders, whereas female leaders have to be both stereotypically female as well as stereotypically leader-like.

Thatcher's Policy Composite

Economic Philosophy

"The masochist in all men responds to the aggressive woman, and recognizes that her charm lies in the appearance of velvet and the reality of iron. Political power will never be sustained by the woman who is a frump."[8] This is recipe for a certain kind of woman, just as it is recipe for a certain kind of man. A woman with strong, even judgmental, policy positions can win, but her path will inevitably be more complicated than a similarly situated man's.

Stereotypes play into this manner of thinking, and society — spun by a like-minded media (not to mention, whoever the opposition happens to be) — is often too willing to hold women to a different standard. Even in recent years, decades after Thatcher, we have seen strong female leaders such as Hillary Rodham Clinton, Sonia Gandhi, Condoleeza Rice and Indra Nooyi endure challenges that equally competitive and aggressive men do not have to.[9] It is almost impossible to endure the glaring spotlight of being expected to be fragile and "feminine" while simultaneously showing policy acumen and the toughness to endure the hurly-burly of a rough and tumble, incompassionate political universe.

Thatcher subtly fused her sex, and the strong matriarchal authority derived from it, with her policy's philosophical foundations and began giving speeches like this one:

> The economic success of the Western world is a product of its moral philosophy and practice. *The economic results are better because the moral philosophy is superior.* Choice is the essence of ethics: if there were no choice, there would be no ethics, no good, no evil; good and evil have meaning only insofar as man is free to choose.[10]

AND RESEARCH 209 (John Wiley and Sons, 2011) (explaining that gender differences of what the public expects "may be intensified at the top.").

[8] See A. Burgess, "Charms of Mrs. Thatcher."
[9] See, *e.g.*, B. Reskin, "What's the Difference? A Comment on Deborah Rhode's 'The Difference 'Difference' Makes'" 112 *in* D. L. Rhode, THE DIFFERENCE 'DIFFERENCE' MAKES: WOMEN IN LEADERSHIP (Stanford University Press, 2003) ("men have more flexible jobs, higher rates of promotion, and more authority on the job.").
[10] M. Thatcher, Speech to Zurich Economic Society ("The New Renaissance"), The University of Zurich, Zurich, Switzerland (March 14, 1977).

Had a white male delivered the same words, he most likely would have been pilloried for Occidental-minded racism. Not only did Thatcher get away with it, she was also praised for her common sense vision. Thatcher was able to play on the "woman complex" successfully. This was the combination of a nanny state-*style* with the *substance* of anything but. From Thatcher's story, as much as we can appreciate the importance of ideas, not an insignificant take-away is that method and approach matter. Had Thatcher's ideas been delivered by a party not nearly as well-attuned to the art of persuasion, in all its forms (and not limited to the verbal), Thatcher may not have become Thatcher — and remained so, years after leaving office.

Thatcher sold many of Great Britain's nationalized industries back to private investors and cut taxes. Thatcher's influences were monetarist thinking and Milton Friedman-type economists, who urged governments to control the money supply rather than work to control demand. To a large extent, Thatcher broke the power of the trade unions, notably in the mining, print and shipbuilding industries and the public sector. Due to her uncompromising leadership style, she became known as the "Iron Lady."

The Falklands

A defining component of the Iron Lady's military legacy, of course, was the Falklands War. In April 1982, the prevailing military junta in Argentina invaded the U.K.-controlled Falkland Islands and South Georgia, thereby inducing the Falklands War. Thatcher had hit upon a landmark test of her tenure. Thatcher chaired a minuscule, informal War Cabinet (different from her usual Cabinet) to control the direction and discharge of this military action. By early April 1982, Thatcher's War Cabinet had dispatched a naval force to regain the islands for the United Kingdom.

Deeply controversial at the time, the 1982 war over the ownership of the Falkland Islands between Great Britain and Argentina allowed Thatcher to show her martial side. When Argentina invaded the Falklands, the United States found itself in a difficult situation, as both Great Britain and Argentina were its allies and trade partners. The United States initially attempted to broker a settlement, but Mrs. Thatcher rejected this compromise, thus cementing her reputation as the Uncompromiser-in-Chief. Upon this, the United States supported Britain with intelligence, not to mention the supply of advanced AIM-9L Sidewinder missiles. This invasion was preceded, and perhaps even encouraged, when Thatcher withdrew the Royal Navy's Antarctic ship HMS Endurance from the South Atlantic, thus giving Argentina what they thought was a free hand to invade.

This is where both Thatcher's *rhetoric* ("Where there is discord, may we bring harmony. Where there is error, may we bring truth. Where there is doubt, may we bring faith. And where there is despair, may we bring hope," "The lady's not for turning" or "Let Labour's Orwellian nightmare of the Left be a spur for us to dedicate with a new urgency our every ounce of energy and moral strength to rebuild the fortunes of this free nation," for example)[11] and her actions began to imitate that of a mother swan trying to protect her cygnets, Gloriana protecting her subjects from the wicked Spanish Armada or whatever other metaphor one elects to use. Thatcher spoke both like a warrior ready to go to battle as well as a peace-maker holding a dove in her hands, much like the Americans' eagle emblem with the same somewhat paradoxical but ultimately reconcilable message. The Prime Minister instantly declared her powerful intention to regain the islands and dispatched a naval task force.

With help from the Chilean President Pinochet (later to be tried as a war criminal for other transgressions) and, far more furtively, Thatcher's ally Ronald Reagan, the British forces quickly recaptured the Falklands. The confrontation that had had the potential to tear the British public apart melted away. From the war emerged a resurgence of popular rejoicing and patriotic enthusiasm, and of course Thatcher's mandate to allow council housing tenants to buy their homes. The Labour opposition was hopelessly mired with in-fighting, delivering for Thatcher a landslide victory in the June 1983 general election. The conflict also led to a strong friendship with the Chilean leader Augusto Pinochet after Chile helped Britain in the conflict.

Pinochet

The hostilities lasted only a few months. Argentina succumbed on 14 June, but Britain did suffer the deaths of 255 servicemen and 3 Falkland Islanders. In contrast, Argentina's fatalities numbered 649, half of whom were the direct result of the torpedoing and sinking by the nuclear submarine HMS Conqueror of ARA General Belgrano in May. Mrs. Thatcher was castigated by the media and some special interest groups for letting diplomatic relations as well as the Falklands' defense become fraught with ineffectiveness. She was also chastised for the military decision to sink the General Belgrano.

---

[11] "1980: Thatcher 'not for turning,'" October 10, 1980, *available at*
<http://news.bbc.co.uk/onthisday/hi/dates/stories/october/10/newsid_2541000/2541071.stm>.

Ultimately, however, she was regarded to have earned her military commander *bona fides*, along the likes of her political hero, Winston Churchill. The comparison would be repeated over and over again on issue after issue. The Falklands victory and economic recuperation led to Thatcher's electoral victory in 1983. It did not hurt that the Labour Party was hopelessly divided and rather leaderless. Thatcher began to call this phenomenon the "Falklands Spirit." Some commentators and historians even suggest that Thatcher began to see the value of quick, rapid-fire choices made by the War Cabinet than the slower, more deliberative and sometimes convoluted peacetime Cabinet decisions.[12] A permanent switch, though, would have been constitutionally unthinkable and perniciously Cromwellian.[13]

Privatisation

On the social front, in 1986, Thatcher's government proscribed the promotion of homosexuality in state schools. Her actions and the philosophy leading to those actions were hailed as morally courageous and almost maternally solicitous by conservative feminists and likeminded social groups. Thatcher followed the same basic strategy when she "emancipated" trade union members by forcing union leaders to hold more democratic, secret ballot elections rather than employ any manner of coercive or wink-and-nod tactics.[14] Her chief foes in this conflict were the leaders of the National Miners' Union (NUM). Thatcher enjoyed looking like a mother-figure, and she played not only on the psyche of the dishevelled school children looking for a strong mother figure and in some cases mother substitute but also on the Virgin Mary-doting-on-Christ-Child theme.

Even Jim Prior's Employment Protection Bill as well as the civil and *criminal* law means Thatcher used (though she downplayed the criminal law usage to tame the unions) did not doom Mrs. Thatcher.[15] The tough love could be contextualized and understood better; the medicine certainly went down easier. The most ironic aspect of the whole era, now surreal, is that this late 1978-early 1979 "winter of discontent" induced, or at least not destroyed, by Mrs. Thatcher negatively affected almost everyone except Mrs. Thatcher herself. She came out on top politically. Whether it was her style, her media spin, admiration of her strength, or just politics taking its time to catch up with her slowly is a harder question and one upon which historians differ.

Undoubtedly the miners' strike was the largest confrontation ever to occur between the unions and Mrs. Thatcher. In March 1984, the National Coal Board (NCB) proposed to shut down 20 of

---

[12] M. Hastings & S. Jenkins, BATTLE FOR THE FALKLANDS 145 (Macmillan, 2010).
[13] Oliver Cromwell, Lord Protector and creator of the English Commonwealth, was instrumental in executing the Stuart monarch Charles I in 1649.
[14] C. Howell, TRADE UNIONS AND THE STATE: THE CONSTRUCTION OF INDUSTRIAL RELATIONS INSTITUTIONS IN BRITAIN, 1890-2000 187 *et seq.* (Princeton University Press, 2007).
[15] C. Wigley, BRITISH TRADE UNIONS, 1945-1995 93 (Manchester University Press, 1997).

the 174 publicly-owned mines and erase 20,000 jobs (out of 187,000), or 10.6%. Two-thirds of all British miners, led by the National Union of Mineworkers (NUM) under the famous or infamous Arthur Scargill, put down their tools as a note of protest. In her usual combative style, Thatcher refused even to meet with Scargill, let alone countenance the union's demands. She went further and compared the miners' dispute to the Falklands War, stating in a 1984 speech: "We had to fight the enemy without in the Falklands. We always have to be aware of the enemy within, which is much more difficult to fight and more dangerous to liberty." Notice, in Thatcher's words, the admonition to Britannia's prodigal or otherwise errant sons, a call to punish or even to ostracise them from society in some shape.

After a year of strikes, around the March of 1985, the leaders of the NUM retreated without a deal. The economic cost was estimated to be at least £1.5 billion. Indeed, some economists attributed the decline of the British pound against the U.S. dollar to the export decline caused by the strike. Thatcher shut down 25 unprofitable coal mines in 1985. The remaining ones were privatised in 1994. The ultimate shutting down of 150 coal mines, some of which were not necessarily sustaining losses, caused the loss of tens of thousands of jobs.

Another point about Thatcher's character emerges here: Miners were part of the anti-Heath constituency who had caused his political decline, which now gave Mrs. Thatcher all the more reason to succeed. Thatcher wanted to show up Heath but, even more, Thatcher wanted to substantiate a sameness feminist slogan: "Whatever he can do, I can do better."[16] Thatcher's initially-dubious tactics included making ready fuel stocks, selecting a strong union-busting official (Ian MacGregor), and making certain that police officers were sufficiently trained and empowered with riot-annihilating gear. It will not be known for decades how far Thatcher actually had empowered them to go in order to crush a potential impediment. Thatcher won the fight and she won the day.

Indeed, the number of stoppages reached 4,583 in 1979 (the zenith). This is when a cumulative 29 million working days were lost. In 1984, the year of the miner strike, there were 1,221, resulting in the loss of more than 27 million working days. Stoppages then fell steadily throughout the rest of Thatcher's premiership; in 1990 there were 630 and fewer than 2 million working days lost, and subsequently continued to fall. Trade union membership too declined, from 13.5 million (1979) to fewer than 10 million by 1990. The British trade union model evolved and, some would argue, was damaged by Mrs. Thatcher.

The maternal image again played up in Thatcher's dealings with the economists (and experts generally). Thatcher claimed a common-sense vision of enacting the right policy that would preclude the disincentives and promote the incentives. Thatcher saw the pernickety "rational

---

[16] The adage actually came from the Irving Berlin's 1946 song "Anything You Can Do" for the Broadway musical, *Annie Get Your Gun*.

actor" model to be clueless and often misguided.[17] Most famously, only about two economists overtly supported, while 364 opposed, Thatcher's tax-raising measure as the recession of the early 1980s deepened. By 1982, the U.K. started experiencing some signs of economic recovery, with inflation dropping to 8.6% from the earlier 18%, though unemployment was over 3 million for the first time since the Great Depression.

By 1983, total economic growth was stronger, and inflation as well as mortgage rates were low, even though output in the manufacturing sector had dropped by 30% since 1978 and unemployment continued to remain high, reaching its zenith at 3.3 million in 1984.[18] By 1987, however, unemployment was decreasing, the economy was stable and powerful, and inflation happened to be low.[19] It is anyone's (educated) guess how much these changes had to do with Mrs. Thatcher's policies or other variables. As with other politicians, Thatcher got significant amounts of both the credit and the blame.

Regarding privatisation, after Prime Minister Thatcher's 1983 election the sale of government utilities sped up. Thatcher raised £29 billion from the sale of nationalized industries, and another £18 billion from the sale of council houses. This privatisation process, especially preparing nationalised industries for privatisation, was credited by the Thatcher government claimed as greatly contributing to significant improvements in output, performance and labour productivity. The overall economic premise of Thatcher's economic philosophy, one supported by conservative intellectuals on both sides of the Atlantic, is that

> markets operate at a position very near to that which might be called 'efficient' – efficient given the costs that firms must face. It further follows from the proposition, again given the presumption of general competitiveness, that actions taken in the market by a single firm generally represent a means for advancing the interests of the firm by providing value to consumers. Put conversely, if a firm's practices did not provide value to consumers, the firm would fail in the competitive battle.[20]

---

[17] J. Blundell, MARGARET THATCHER: A PORTRAIT OF THE IRON LADY 95-96 (Algora Publishing, 2008) [J. Blundell, MARGARET THATCHER].
[18] B. Jones, et al., POLITICS UK 705-06 (Pearson Education, 2007); R. Toye & J. Gottlieb, MAKING REPUTATIONS: POWER, PERSUASION AND THE INDIVIDUAL IN MODERN BRITISH POLITICS 156-170 (I.B. Tauris Publishing, 2005) [R. Toye & J. Gottlieb, MAKING REPUTATIONS]; D. Yergin & Joseph Stanislaw, THE COMMANDING HEIGHTS: THE BATTLE FOR THE WORLD ECONOMY 14 *et seq.* (Simon and Schuster, 2002); H. Norpoth, CONFIDENCE REGAINED: ECONOMICS, MRS. THATCHER, AND THE BRITISH VOTER 9 (University of Michigan Press, 1992).
[19] R. Toye & J. Gottlieb, MAKING REPUTATIONS, *supra*, at 156-58.
[20] See G. L. Priest, *The Abiding Influence of* The Antitrust Paradox*: An Essay in Honor of Robert H. Bork*, 31 HARV. J. L. & PUB. POL'Y 455, 458 (2008) [G. L. Priest, *The Abiding Influence of* The Antitrust Paradox]; see also R. H. Bork, THE ANTITRUST PARADOX: A POLICY AT WAR WITH ITSELF (Free Press, 1978) (grounding the new competition law in consumer welfare); F. H. Easterbrook, *The Chicago School and Exclusionary Conduct*, 31 HARV. J. L. & PUB. POL'Y 439 (2008); R. A. Skitol, *The Shifting Sands of Antitrust Policy: Where it has Been,*

Certain privatised industries including the basic utilities (gas, water, and electricity), were of course natural monopolies for which privatisation meant marginal increase in competition. The privatised industries that demonstrated improvement often did so while still under public ownership. British Steel, for instance, became far more profitable while remaining a nationalised industry under the Thatcher government chairmanship of Ian MacGregor, who refused to buckle under union pressure to close plants and half the workforce.

The answer then might just be effective management rather than privatisation, but of course the Thatcherites claim that long-term effective management is unsustainable as a publicly owned industry. Regulation was also significantly expanded to compensate for the loss of direct government control, with the foundation of regulatory bodies. There is a need to point out that regulatory bodies are not that different from legislative government control, and they do not necessarily work.. It must also be pointed that Thatcherites are correct that the problem is not that the consumer is "stupid";[21] rather what few seem to have spotted is that the issue is one of informational asymmetry and the lack of time that might allow the "rational" consumer (one without significant resources) to deduce the preferred course of action accurately. On the contrary, this kind of argument in fact presupposes that the consumer is highly rational and intelligent — and far from "stupid."

Moreover, lawyers must easily see through this regulatory ruse to some extent because regulatory control is not, in practice, that different from direct ownership and control. From the perspective of the subjected industry, there is still a loss of autonomy or agency. This begs the question: To what extent were these reforms just cosmetic? Government interference with the control of a private corporation may in some cases convert "subsequent acts of the private corporation" into "acts of the State."[22]

There was no obvious, unequivocal pattern concerning competition, regulation, and

---

Where it is Now, Where it Will be in its Third Century, 9 CORNELL L. & PUB. POL'Y 239, 248 (1999).

[21] See, e.g., Jon D. Hanson & Douglas A. Kysar, *Taking Behavioralism Seriously: The Problem of Market Manipulation*, 74 N.Y.U. L. REV. 630, 633 (1999) ("These cognitive illusions—sometimes referred to as 'biases'—are not limited to the uneducated or unintelligent, and they are not readily capable of being unlearned. Instead, they affect us all with uncanny consistency and unflappable persistence." (footnotes omitted)); Christine Jolls et al., *A Behavioral Approach to Law and Economics*, 50 STAN. L. REV. 1471, 1541 (1998) ("In its normative orientation, conventional law and economics is often strongly antipaternalistic. . . . [B]ounded rationality pushes toward a sort of anti-antipaternalism—a skepticism about antipaternalism, but not an affirmative defense of paternalism."); Russell B. Korobkin & Thomas S. Ulen, *Law and Behavioral Science: Removing the Rationality Assumption from Law and Economics*, 88 CAL. L. REV. 1051, 1085 (2000).

[22] See D. D. Caron, "The Basis of Responsibility: Attribution and Other Trans-Substantive Rules" *in* THE IRAN-UNITED STATES CLAIMS TRIBUNAL: ITS CONTRIBUTION TO THE LAW OF STATE RESPONSIBILITY 168 (1998); see also R. Lillich, ed., INTERNATIONAL LAW OF STATE RESPONSIBILITY FOR INJURIES TO ALIENS 270-3 (1983); insurrections, civil wars, revolutions and armed external intervention have generated cases like *United States-Iran Hostages Case*, 19 ILM 553 (1980), or *Nicaragua v. United States*, 25 ILM 1023 (1986); C. F. Amerasinghe, STATE RESPONSIBILITY FOR INJURIES TO ALIENS 152-6 (Clarendon Press, 1967).

performance among the privatised industries; in most cases Thatcher's policy held that privatisation benefited consumers by keeping or lowering prices and improving efficiency (by limiting bureaucratic complacency). With greater consumer options, there could be threats that the critical mass would shift. In actuality, though, it is difficult to say if the results, on the whole, showed that the policies *work in the long run.* To be sure, Thatcher herself refused to go the full extent of the new competition law developments (championed by the Chicago School) when she refused to privatise the railway industry, something that her immediate successor John Major would do with largely calamitous results. Specifically, Thatcher did not quite accept the new arguments that "barriers to entry" do not exist or ultimately benefit consumers or that "small business need not be protected against large business."[23]

Northern Ireland

We cannot underestimate how Northern Ireland tested Thatcher as a politician and as a human being. Northern Ireland's Catholic/Protestant divisions were a thorn (and in some ways still are). In 1980 and 1981, Provisional Irish Republican Army (IRA) and Irish National Liberation Army (INLA) prisoners in Northern Ireland's Maze Prison conducted several hunger strikes in order to get back the status of political prisoners; this status had been taken away from them in 1976 under Labour. Bobby Sands, whose memorial still stands in Belfast, commenced the 1981 strike, declaring that he would fast until death unless prison inmates were granted better living and political conditions.[24]

---

[23] See G. L. Priest, *The Abiding Influence of* The Antitrust Paradox, *supra*, at 460.
[24] See B. O'Leary, *Mission Accomplished? Looking Back at the IRA*, 1 FIELD DAY REV. 217, 219 (2005); B. Kissane, EXPLAINING IRISH DEMOCRACY 156ff (Dublin, 2002); K. Toolis, REBEL HEARTS: JOURNEYS WITHIN THE IRA'S SOUL 28ff (London, 1995); S. Cronin, IRISH NATIONALISM: A HISTORY OF ITS ROOTS AND IDEOLOGY (London, 1980).

The Bobby Sands mural in Belfast

Thatcher vociferously refused to tolerate a return to political status for the prisoners, declaring "Crime is crime is crime; it is not political," but the British government *furtively* contacted the higher-ups of the IRA in a strong effort to bring the hunger strikes to an end.[25] Upon the deaths of Sands and several others, certain (though not nearly all) rights were restored to paramilitary prisoners; nonetheless there was no official status recognition. Indeed, Northern Irish violence worsened greatly during the hunger strikes.

Thatcher's IRA enemies had it in for her. She was almost assassinated in an IRA attempt at a Brighton hotel on October 12, 1984. In the attempt, five people were killed, including Government Minister John Wakeham's wife. Thatcher was staying at the hotel to attend the Tory Party Conference, which she insisted should open as scheduled the following day. It was going to be business as usual, possibly the most Thatcher'esque statement that could ever be made. Thatcher was sending a strong message even by that non-move of postponing or calling off the conference. She delivered her speech, a decision that was strongly supported across the political spectrum and enhanced her general popularity. There is nothing quite like a tragedy to unify the bickering factions.

Thatcher's reputation as an unflinchingly strong political leader won her political points, and her reputation as an unflinchingly strong *woman* political leader won her political points and a place in history. We will never know for certain the precise extent to which the call of history was on Thatcher's mind when she showed her characteristic insouciance and her devil-may-care attitude.

In November 1981 Thatcher and Irish Taoiseach Garret FitzGerald decided to establish and assemble the Anglo-Irish Inter-Governmental Council, a proactive and interactive forum where discussions, deliberations and meetings between the governments could take place. On November 15, 1985, Thatcher and FitzGerald signed the Hillsborough Anglo-Irish Agreement, which had the distinction of being the first instance that Britain had given the Republic of Ireland something of an advisory capacity in Northern Ireland's governance and administration. It must be noted that this decision was not without costs: as a note of protest, the Ulster Says No movement drew 100,000 people to a Belfast protest rally, Ian Gow resigned as Minister of State in Treasury, and *all* 15 Unionist MPs resigned their seats. The war-ready leader and rebel mother had shown she could also be a peace-maker of startling proportions, perhaps too far out in front politically, at least for the sake of cohesion.

---

[25] See J. Blundell, MARGARET THATCHER, *supra*, at 131 *et seq.*

The Cold War

On foreign relations, Thatcher found a kindred spirit over the issue of breaking the will and economic support of the Communists, particularly the Soviet Union: U.S. President Ronald Reagan. Reagan and Thatcher have historically been credited for bringing down the Berlin Wall and ending the Soviet Union as it had been known, but it remains unclear whether it would or would not have happened under a different chain of events. History's road-not-taken is almost always notoriously impossible to trace.[26]

While it is impossible to fully analyze to what extent the fall of Soviet communism and the aftermath (*perestroika*, etc.) can be attributed to Prime Minister Thatcher, it is nonetheless obvious that some credit is owed to her, even if it was just as a function of timing (she embraced the opportunity when she saw it and made more of it than was immediately evident could be the case). Thatcher took office in the 1970s, the penultimate decade in the four decade long history of the Cold War. Thatcher became closely aligned with American policies and particularly with President Reagan, an alliance grounded as much in a mutual distrust and dislike of communism as it was on shared economic interests. After all, in October 1983, when Reagan invaded Grenada, Thatcher powerfully and vociferously opposed him. Scholars such as Judith Resnik identify such attitudes of "form[ing] connections and groups" and "shar[ing] work stemm[ing] from" the constructive motivation "to alter the shape and understanding" of politics, life, and culture peculiarly feminine.[27]

In Thatcher's first year as Prime Minister she had indeed supported the North Atlantic Treaty Organization's (NATO) decision to deploy United States nuclear cruise missiles in Western Europe, and she had even actively enabled the United States to station 160 cruise missiles in the United Kingdom. She had stood her ground despite massive opposition by the lobbying efforts of the powerful Campaign for Nuclear Disarmament. Thatcher subsequently purchased from Reagan and the United States, as part of her pre-emptive strategy, the Trident nuclear missile submarine system. This striking move tripled Britain's nuclear forces, thereby costing more than £12 billion.[28]

Thatcher's preference to stay the course was tested (and so was her commitment to military commitments and alliances with the United States) in the Westland affair of January 1986. At that time, Thatcher allowed the struggling helicopter manufacturer Westland to reject an acquisition offer from the Italian company Agusta in favour of the management's preferred course of action. Thatcher's own Defense Secretary, Michael Heseltine, who had been a champion of the Agusta option, resigned to register his opposition to Thatcher on what he saw as

---

[26] C. Berlinski, THERE IS NO ALTERNATIVE: WHY MARGARET THATCHER MATTERS 47 *et seq*. (Basic Books, 2008).
[27] J. Resnik, "Women, Meeting (Again), in and Beyond the United States" 205 *in* D. L. Rhode, THE DIFFERENCE 'DIFFERENCE' MAKES: WOMEN IN LEADERSHIP (Stanford University Press, 2003).
[28] The 2012 cost would be approximately £17.64 billion.

this significant issue.

Other Foreign Relations

What of apartheid South Africa? Despite maintaining her anti-apartheid stance, Thatcher believed the sanctions imposed on South Africa by the Commonwealth and the European Community were ineffective. She tried to continue trade and investments with South Africa's apartheid government while convincing the regime to repudiate apartheid.[29] Thatcher's public and ostensible argument was not that different from her economic policy premise: boycotts hurt the British manufacturing works as well as poor, black South Africans. The rationale was grounded in consumer and plebeian welfare. Thatcher, perhaps due to her own personal IRA experience in Brighton, was antagonized by the tactics of the African National Congress (ANC), which Thatcher may have dismissed as "a typical terrorist organisation."[30]

This impatience with agents Thatcher saw as ill in method and form as well as an effort to be expedient applied also to the Khmer Rouge government of Cambodia. Thatcher supported their retaining their United Nations seat ("the more reasonable" of the choices, she said) *after* the Cambodian-Vietnamese War saw to their ouster from Cambodia.[31]

Now we come to the Libya and Middle East issue. In April 1986, Thatcher permitted U.S. fighter and bomber jets to use the U.K.'s Royal Air Force bases to bomb of Libya in order to retaliate against the alleged Libyan bombing of a Berlin nightclub. Both Thatcher and Reagan had referred to the United Nations Charter's Article 51 allowing nations to defend themselves, sometimes pre-emptively. The move was extremely damaging and unpopular with the British public. By this time, the public was a weary one, unwilling to give Mrs. Thatcher the benefit of doubt any longer. When, as we soon shall see, she did fall from grace, it was after 11 and a half years in political office and the public patience was wearing thin. Had she served much longer, a long-tenure precedent might have been set that made room for casual corruption and other political machine-like behaviour.[32]

When Iraq's Saddam Hussein invaded Kuwait in August 1990 (mainly for oil — an interest both for the United States and the United Kingdom), Thatcher powerfully urged United States President George H. W. Bush to intervene, specifically to deploy American troops in the Middle

---

[29] T. Bell & D. B. Ntsebeza, UNFINISHED BUSINESS: SOUTH AFRICA, APARTHEID, AND TRUTH 77 (Verso, 2003); J. Gardner, POLITICIANS AND APARTHEID: TRAILING IN THE PEOPLE'S WAKE 119 (HSRC Press, 1997); S. R. Lewis, THE ECONOMICS OF APARTHEID 38-52 (Council on Foreign Relations, 1990).

[30] G. Howe, CONFLICT OF LOYALTY 123-4 (Macmillan, 1994). Prime Minister Thatcher's own Foreign Secretary, Geoffrey Howe so articulated.

[31] T. Fawthorp, GETTING AWAY WITH GENOCIDE?: ELUSIVE JUSTICE AND THE KHMER ROUGE 69-72 (UNSW Press, 2005); C. Etcheson, AFTER THE KILLING FIELDS: LESSONS FROM THE CAMBODIAN GENOCIDE 185 (Greenwood Publishing Group, 2005).

[32] It is true that Prime Minister Tony Blair (1997-2007) also served a long tenure but his tenure did not exceed Thatcher's in length.

East to oust the Iraqi military from Kuwait. Despite Bush's reluctance, Thatcher pushed him very hard and eventually won his support. In this endeavour, Thatcher provided the United States with British military forces to the international coalition in the build-up to the Gulf War, but she had resigned from office (partly *because* of this particular engagement, which may well have been a bridge too far) by the time hostilities began on January 17, 1991.

As we have seen many times over, Thatcher the peace-maker travelled alongside Thatcher the martial leader and war-monger, one of the many internal contradictions that makes the former Prime Minister's composite so interesting to study. Margaret Thatcher was among the first Western leaders to encourage to the Soviet reformer Mikhail Gorbachev. Many other Western leaders were rather lukewarm or taking longer to warm up to Gorabchev. Subequent to the Reagan–Gorbachev summit and Gorbachev's domestic reforms, in 1988 Thatcher announced that the Cold War was effectively over and that the West and the Soviet Union now enjoyed a "new relationship much wider than the Cold War ever was." Initially Thatcher strongly opposed to Germany's reunification, predicting to Gorbachev that it "would lead to a change to post-war borders, and we cannot allow that because such a development would undermine the stability of the whole international situation and could endanger our security."

Thatcher was thinking strategically. She was concerned that a whole, united Germany would most likely choose the side of the Soviet Union and reject the NATO. Thatcher was, however, a supporter of Croatian and Slovenian independence. In a 1991 interview, Thatcher criticized the West for failing to recognize the secessionist Slovenian and Croatian republics as independent nations. Thatcher also argued that the Western powers ought to equipped Slovenia and Croatia with weapons after they were attacked by the Serbian-Yugoslav forces. Was this impartial? How would Thatcher the Prime Minister have responded had Scotland or any other part of the United Kingdom wanted total independence?[33] We may surmise that Mrs. Thatcher would not have been best pleased.

European Union

Above all else, the foreign policy stances and decisions Thatcher took and made vis-à-vis the European Community indicate that she was extraordinarily protective of British sovereignty in all matters. Her pungent dislike of European integration became ever more obvious during her Prime Minister years. The moderate stances she had once taken on this question now were miles apart from the uncompromising stance she took after her third election victory in 1987.

---

[33] See, *e.g.*, R. Legvold, "Book Review: Slaughterhouse: Bosnia and the Failure of the West," *Foreign Affairs*, May/June 1995, *available at* <www.foreignaffairs.com/articles/50892/robert-legvold/slaughterhouse-bosnia-and-the-failure-of-the-west>. D. Rieff, SLAUGHTERHOUSE: BOSNIA AND THE FAILURE OF THE WEST 14 *et seq.* (Simon & Schuster, 1996); R. Ali & Lifschultz, WHY BOSNIA?: WRITINGS ON THE BALKAN WAR 112-14 (Pamphleteer's Press, 1993).

Memorably, Thatcher explained her disagreement with almost every proposal from the European Community (EC), precursor to the European Union, for a more federal structure and greater centralisation to govern policy choices.

Back in the days of the 1975 national referendum, Thatcher and the Tories had supported (some might say, championed) British membership of the European Communities, but her views on this topic were not boundless. Thatcher saw it as a narrow question, believing that the EC's role should be confined to making sure intra-European free trade and stable, strong competition existed. Thatcher was concerned that the EC's *approach* as well as its *substantive goals* would bring about the bigger government and regulatory state she was attempting to steer the United Kingdom away from.

In 1988, Thatcher memorably remarked: "We have not successfully rolled back the frontiers of the state in Britain, only to see them re-imposed at a European level, with a European super-state exercising a new dominance from Brussels." Thatcher's now-famous Parliamentary diatribe of "No, No, No" to greater EC dominance still rings. Thatcher also was strongly opposed to the United Kingdom's membership of the Exchange Rate Mechanism, a forerunner to European Monetary Union. Her view was that such a move would limit the options for the British economy. Again, Prime Minister Thatcher stood her ground despite arguments to the contrary advanced by her Chancellor of the Exchequer Nigel Lawson and Geoffrey Howe. Nonetheless, her successor John Major convinced Thatcher to join in October 1990 — albeit at what turned out to be rather high an exchange rate.

Her Fall and Her Resurrection

Thatcher in 1990

Thatcher had led the Tories to victory in three general elections (1979, 1983 and 1987), but by 1990, Thatcher's popularity was decreasing tremendously and there were calls from within her own party for her to resign from office. She was challenged for the party leadership and just failed to gain the necessary majority in the first election, despite attaining a greater number of votes than her chief rival Michael Heseltine. Upon being persuaded by colleagues that she would narrowly fail, Thatcher decided to drop out of the second ballot and resigned as party leader on November 22, 1990.

John Major won the Tory leadership vote, and then was appointed to succeed Thatcher as Prime Minister. Thatcher was the longest serving British Prime Minister in more than a century and a half and found herself in a pantheon of two, just with the celebrated Winston Churchill. Together they remain regarded, by friend and foe alike, two of the most influential British premiers of the twentieth century. The complexity of sex played into Thatcher's political operations. There was no precedent. It was a game that she had to win once and keep winning.

Arguably Thatcher's most interesting post-Premier action came in August 1992, when Thatcher called for NATO to put a stop to the Serbian assault on Goražde and Sarajevo to end ethnic cleansing. She compared the Bosnian situation to "the worst excesses of the Nazis," and deemed this to be close to a "holocaust."[34] Thatcher made several House of Lords speeches — she had been created Baroness Thatcher —criticising the Maastricht Treaty,[35] stating bluntly (and perhaps inappropriately and presumptuously[36]) "I could never have signed this treaty." Even at her 80th birthday gala, attended by such luminaries as the Queen and then-Prime Minister Tony Blair, Mrs. Thatcher remained sharp, witty and opinionated and remained, as ever, not just a certain kind of woman but a certain kind of British woman.

Mrs. Thatcher remained a mainstay in affairs until 2002, delivering speeches, writing her own memoirs, and perhaps most famously writing about political statesmanship in *Statecraft: Strategies for a Changing World*, which she dedicated to Ronald Reagan. That all changed after she began suffering strokes in 2002, which limited her public appearances and speaking. Now well into her twilight, Thatcher is in a state of frail health, and it has been widely reported that she is suffering from dementia. Not even the Iron Lady could withstand old age.

Thatcher may be personally fading from the scene, but her reputation and legacy have never been stronger. Although *The Iron Lady* has brought her entire life, including her fight with dementia, back into the public consciousness, it's her political legacy and philosophy that have truly made her a living legend in the 21st century. In particular, her championing of free-market philosophies and her railing against government intervention at all levels, including against the European Union, have made her an icon of political conservatives across the West, elevating her onto a pedestal alongside kindred spirit Ronald Reagan. To a lesser degree, Thatcher continues to have critics, who point to high unemployment during her premiership and have charged her with doing "little to advance the political cause of women",

In addition to the legacy she left on Britain and Europe at large, Thatcher's life and career have left a marked legacy on all of the female politicians that have followed her since. Since the Thatcher days, female leaders have had to continue to prove their mettle as dispassionate and yet feminine, ruthless and yet maternal, fiercely intelligent to master every subtle argument and yet uphold the soft, sweeping, broad vision to encourage the troops and boost their morale. For women seeking to follow Thatcher's path, the game is still on.

---

[34] M. Thatcher, "Stop the Excuses. Help Bosnia Now," *New York Times*, August 6, 1992, *available at* <http://query.nytimes.com/gst/fullpage.html?res=9E0CE7DE1731F935A3575BC0A964958260&sec=&spon=&pagewanted=2>.
[35] Treaty on European Union (92/C 191/01),
[36] Thatcher had also not had to face the particular economic and political sanctions that Tony Blair did, on behalf of the United Kingdom.

Made in the USA
Middletown, DE
27 August 2020